THE MUSIC MAKERS

A Brief History of the
Birmingham Triennial Musical Festivals
1784 - 1912
by
Anne Elliott

The Music Makers
A Brief History of the Birmingham Triennial Musical Festivals 1784 - 1912
© 2000 Anne Elliott

ISBN: 07093 0224 X

CIP catalogue record for this book is available from the British Library.

Published by Birmingham Library Services.
Design and Production by CSO Design 0121 303 1986.

CONTENTS

Early 19th Century engraving of St. Philip's Church (later Birmingham Cathedral)

FOREWORD

The Birmingham Triennial Festival, as it grew in stature and fame, mirrored the phenomenal development of a great industrial city: 35,000 people in 1760; over a million by 1931. The city's commercial energies were repeated in a quest for artistic excellence and innovation.

The Triennial was one of the most important international festivals of its day, raising the city's profile in Europe and beyond. Now, while modern Birmingham relies heavily on being an international destination for conferences, trade exhibitions and sports events, one of its continuing attractions is the quality and variety of its musical life, spearheaded by the CBSO.

This book helps us to understand so much about our vibrant community's artistic development. The demise of the Festival at the start of the Great War, though sad, was no tragedy, the city's musical life continuing with renewed vigour thereafter. The Festival Committee's policy of commissioning new work from the best composers of the time has been continued and enhanced across the whole spectrum of arts in the city.

Perhaps, as the twenty-first century dawns, there is room to explore our Festival's legacy. We intend to begin that process in October 2000 with the centenary performance of Elgar's *Dream of Gerontius*.

Simon Halsey

Chorus director, City of Birmingham Symphony Orchestra
Principal conductor, City of Birmingham Touring Opera

A performance of the *The Dream of Gerontius* at the 1909 Festival conducted by Richter

INTRODUCTION

Long before Simon Rattle and the CBSO brought Birmingham to the attention of music lovers across the world, the Triennial Musical Festival gave the city an international artistic reputation. The Festivals ran from 1784 through until 1912 and during the course of its 120-year span, many famous composers were commissioned to write works for the Festival which were performed by the foremost artistes of the day.

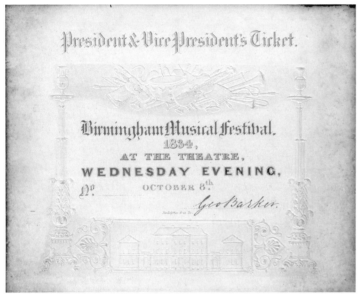

President/Vice President's ticket for Birmingham Music Festival, 8th October 1834

August 1996 saw the 150th anniversary of the first performance of Mendelssohn's oratorio *Elijah* at Birmingham Town Hall as part of the 1846 Triennial Festival. To celebrate this event, Birmingham Central Library staged an exhibition during August and September 1996 entitled '*The Music Makers - the Birmingham Triennial Musical Festival 1846-1912*'.

The history of the Festival was told on a series of panels as the background to a large number of exhibits which included items relating to Mendelssohn, Gounod, Dvorak and Elgar from Birmingham Central Library collections and other sources.

This publication is based on the text used for the exhibition and as such it reflects the particular areas of interest which were highlighted there. The early history of the Festival is only sketched and although the rest of the text is a chronological survey, there is no attempt to mention each Festival in turn. Most attention is given to particular composers and their work for the Triennial Festivals and to some of the Festival administrators who worked with them.

The Birmingham Festival Choral Society provided the nucleus of the choir used at each Festival from 1846 and in fact has long outlived the Festivals, continuing a successful independent existence. Its members and the other performers at the Festivals were essential to their continuing success but they do not feature significantly in this account. However, information on the Society is available elsewhere.[1]

A comprehensive history of the Festivals has still to be written and remains a distant prospect, while one of the most valuable sources of information has still to be rediscovered: the minutes of the various Festival Committees disappeared some time after the final Festival in 1912 and apart from a few tantalising quotes in other sources, remain unknown. The Music section of Birmingham Central Library would be most interested in any information anybody has regarding these papers, or indeed any other papers, ephemera or memorabilia associated with the Triennial Festivals.

BEGINNINGS

The first Birmingham Triennial Musical Festival was held in September 1784 when £703 was raised to supplement the income of the General Hospital (then a charitable institution which had opened in 1779).[2]

Various one-off musical events had been held previously whenever the hospital's finances had been in particular need of help; but 1784 marked the start of a festival which was held regularly every three years with the stated aim of contributing money towards the ever-increasing cost of the hospital's services.

At this time the Festivals were held in either the Theatre, New Street or St. Philip's Church (later Birmingham Cathedral) and consisted largely of music by Handel: not only *The Messiah* but also *Acis and Galatea*, *Joshua*, *Israel in Egypt*, *Solomon*, and *Theodora*. The concerts were given over the course of three days and concert-goers were also able to enjoy balls which were held in the evening.

The Festivals developed during the early nineteenth century to include music by Mozart, Beethoven, Weber, Rossini, and Spohr - reflecting contemporary developments in music. The receipts continued to increase although the amount of profit available for the General Hospital did not grow at the same rate, as running the Festival became more expensive.

The Festival scheduled for 1832 was delayed by two years to allow all the musical events to take place in the new purpose-built Town Hall. The hall contained an organ built by William Hill, who was to become the foremost English organ-builder. When it was installed the organ was positioned further forward but it was Mendelssohn who suggested that it would sound better if it was moved towards the back of the all to the position it now occupies. It set a trend for concert organs in England and all over the world, and became a vital element in Festival performances. Although the organ has been modified it is still there today in its original case. The 1834 Festival was a considerable success and the Town Hall became the venue for all the subsequent Triennial Festivals.

A commemorative medal struck to celebrate the opening of Birmingham Town Hall in October 1834

FELIX MENDELSSOHN AND BIRMINGHAM

In its new surroundings the Festival was extended to four days and involved a greater number of performers. For the 1834 Festival, the organising committee made their first commission for a new work to be composed. Sigismund Neukomm, a pupil of Haydn and composer of over a thousand works, who was one of the Festival's organists, composed an oratorio *David*. Unfortunately both the composer and the work have long been forgotten. However, this is certainly not the case with the Festival's next commission.

Felix Mendelssohn first appeared in Birmingham in 1837 at the invitation of his friend, and long-time director of the Triennial Festivals, Joseph Moore. Mendelssohn took the proceedings by storm. He conducted a performance of his oratorio *St Paul*, played the organ both as a soloist and as part of the orchestra, and performed the solo part in his second piano concerto - the Festival commission.

A commentator said that the piano concerto:

created intense excitement. As soon as he [Mendelssohn] entered the orchestra, the applause was almost uproarious...[3]

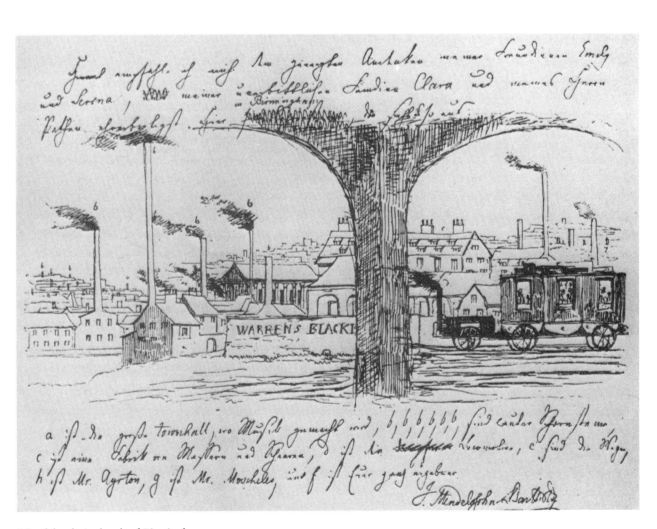

Mendelssohn's sketch of Birmingham

Mendelssohn himself was very pleased with its reception. In a letter dated 4th October 1837 he wrote:

I had such a brilliant success...The applause and shouts at the least glimpse of me...really made me laugh...and a sure proof of my success were the offers made to me on all sides, and of a very different tenor this time from what they were before.[4]

Mendelssohn found the whole experience exhausting, especially as he had to be back in Leipzig immediately for the start of the season.

Both Mendelssohn and his wife were ill in the period leading up to the 1840 Festival, which somewhat limited his involvement. *The Hymn of Praise [Lobgesang]* was given its British première but was not particularly well-received either by the audience or indeed by the composer. What appears to have been a commission for another piano concerto was not completed and Mendelssohn played his first concerto instead.

The next Festival was characterised both by economies of scale and content and by Mendelssohn's absence. It was not surprising that there was a resulting drop in income which made the Festival Committee reconsider its position for the event in 1846.

ELIJAH

On 11th June 1845 the Birmingham Festival Committee passed a resolution:

that it appears to this committee desirable that the services of Dr. Mendelssohn be obtained to act as Conductor at the next Festival; and that he be requested to consider whether he can provide a new oratorio or other music, for the occasion.[5]

Mendelssohn declined to conduct anything other than his own works (as had previously been the case at the Festival) and suggested his friend Moscheles as a replacement. He tentatively accepted the offer of a commission; the invitation revived plans, which he had previously dropped, of composing an oratorio on the subject of Elijah.

However eager he was to write a work for the Festival, Mendelssohn was very busy with his duties in Germany and as early as October 1845 he expressed doubts as to whether he would be able to complete it on time. In December he wrote to Joseph Moore, director of the Festival, offering *Walpurgisnacht* or *A Midsummer Night's Dream* as possible alternatives if the new work was not ready.[6]

However, by 15th January 1846 work on *Elijah* was under way and Mendelssohn asked that Jenny Lind be engaged as the soprano soloist - a request that proved impossible to fulfil. Although progress was slow, Mendelssohn was able to write to Moore in May that:

I write these lines to inform you that I intend to send the whole of the first part of my oratorio to Mr. Moscheles in the course of the next fortnight. It is by far the greater part of the two; the choruses from the second part will be in England towards the beginning of July ... All this, Deo volente. I wish Mr. Bartholomew, in London, who has translated several other vocal pieces of mine, would undertake also this.[7]

Although the second half was despatched as promised in July, some of the chorus parts were not available until three weeks before the performance.

Mendelssohn was paid 200 guineas (£210) for the commission and the same was given to the principal soprano, Maria Caradori - Allan. Joseph Staudigl singing Elijah received a fee of 150 guineas and the organist for the occasion, Henry Gauntlett, £30.

Early rehearsals were held in London and then the composer, his friends, the press, the orchestra and the London contingent of the chorus came to Birmingham on a specially - chartered train. There was an extra rehearsal on the Tuesday evening of the Festival and then on the morning of Wednesday, 26th August, *Elijah* was given its première.

The performance was an outstanding success (with eight numbers being encored immediately) and made a lasting impression on everyone who was there. The Times reported the following day:

The last note of Elijah *was drowned in a long - continued unanimous volley of plaudits, vociferous & deafening. It was as though enthusiasm, long checked, had suddenly burst its bounds and filled the air with shouts of exhultation. Mendelssohn, evidently overpowered, bowed its acknowledgement and quietly descended from his position in the conductor's rostrum; but he was compelled to appear again, amidst renewed cheers and huzzas. Never was there a more thorough and speedy triumph...*

Mendelssohn wrote to his brother:

No work of mine ever went so admirably the first time of execution, or was received with such enthusiasm by both the musicians and the audience, as this oratorio... A young English tenor [Charles Lockey] sang the last air so beautifully, that I was obliged to collect all my energies so as not to be affected, and to continue beating time steadily.[8]

THE BIRMINGHAM MUSICAL FESTIVAL.—THE GREAT MUSIC HALL.—(SEE NEXT PAGE)

Illustrated London News engraving showing the audience in Birmingham Town Hall for the first performance of Mendelssohn's *Elijah* in 1846

He wrote to Joseph Moore:

Indeed, the first performance of my Elijah exceeded all the wishes which a composer may feel at such an important moment, and the evident good-will of all the artists in the orchestra, as well as the kindness with which the audience received the work, will be as long as I live a source of grateful recollection.[9]

After the 1846 Festival, the Committee passed a resolution:

That this Committee, deeply impressed by the unprecedented success of the oratorio Elijah written for this Festival, do return their very cordial and grateful thanks to Dr. Felix Mendelssohn-Bartholdy for a Composition in which the most consummate musical knowledge and the highest intellectual conceptions are displayed; a Composition which will soon be universally known, and not only add to the fame, already so great, of the Author, but tend to exalt the art which he professes, and on which his genius and judgement reflect so much honour.[10]

Elijah was performed at every succeeding Triennial Festival.

THE BIRMINGHAM MANUSCRIPT

Birmingham Central Library now holds the manuscript of Mendelssohn's *Elijah* as performed at the Birmingham Town Hall on 26th August 1846.

The main part of it was written by the copyist Eduard Henschke with autograph annotations by Mendelssohn (eg. indicating Biblical references, and tempo and dynamic markings) and by William Bartholomew, the translator of the text. There are also performance notes by Henry Gauntlett, the

Manuscript full score of *Elijah* used at the first performance in Birmingham in 1846. (Birmingham City Archives MS1721)

organist at the first performance.

The score was sent to England in instalments, starting in May 1846 and finishing less than three weeks before the performance. Mendelssohn neglected to bring an organ part so Henry Gauntlett had to use this score to play from: hence the written notes of registrations and the use of figured bass.

Despite the success of the first performance, Mendelssohn revised *Elijah* extensively and a new version (published in 1847) was subsequently the only one performed. The existence of the original 1846 score was gradually forgotten until rediscovered in the archives of the music publisher Novello in 1986.

The 1846 score was bought at auction by Birmingham City Council in December 1991, with financial assistance from the National Heritage Memorial Fund, and the Museums and Galleries Commission's Special Grant Fund.

A PERIOD OF TRANSITION

The American music educator Lowell Mason visited Birmingham and the Triennial Festival in 1852 as part of a European lecture tour. Although he was generally impressed, he compared the Birmingham Festival to one he had been to in Dusseldorf:

The people ... in Dusseldorf were interested in the festival - indeed it was the people's festival, *and if there were some who could not hear, all took delight in seeing. But* here, *the common people are entirely cut off from the music; it is intended only for the rich, and only they can go to the expense of purchasing admittance. There, the people make their own music;* here, *the greatest performers, vocal and instrumental, the world affords, are brought together, at an enormous expense, to give an exhibition of the triumph of art.*[11]

Mason further justified his view with a description of the audience in the Town Hall for the customary performance of *Elijah*:

The great Hall now presented a most splendid appearance. It seemed as if all the beauty and fashion of the kingdom, all the colors of the rainbow, and all the resources of embellishment, had been called in to enliven and give effect to the brilliant spectacle.[12]

When he first arrived at the Festival, Mason wanted to buy tickets and he describes his encounter with the bureaucracy which was an inevitable part of running such a large and successful musical event:

We went early to procure our tickets, but found a crowd already in the office. ... Some fifteen or eighteen clerks were employed in attending to the calls of purchasers. There was one clerk for selling reserved seats for each morning, and one also for each evening performance; two clerks for unreserved seats, ... two for the sale of programmes, or books of words; besides which, several other officers were employed, giving the whole an air of business almost equal to the stock exchange, Paris.[13]

The principal conductor of the Festival at this time was Michael Costa whose relationship with Birmingham started in 1829 when, as a young composer of nineteen, he performed in one of his own works. He became the Festival's principal conductor in 1849 (after Mendelssohn's death) and held the post until 1882. He was also commissioned to write two cantatas for the Festival: *Eli* in 1855 and *Naaman* in 1864. Both works were initially very popular, particularly two choral marches which were performed by amateur choirs and orchestras and which were even issued in tonic sol-fa.

However, they gradually disappeared into obscurity and only a recent comment from a music historian gives some idea of their content:

Michael Costa's Eli, *first performed at the Festival in 1855, is a work to gladden the hearts of all who love Victorian curiosities. Never before or since can the church and the opera house have joined hands in such amazing but vital incongruity.*

Costa's real self emerges against his will in the passages of refined early Verdi and Meyerbeer (with lavish use of brass) but he constantly attempts to disguise it beneath a coat of applied Spohr and Mendelssohn in a naively touching effort to be reverent.

This Janus-like attitude does not preclude the gestation of some very fine music (see 'Hear my prayer, O God').[14]

Photomontage of artists and composers from the 1867 Festival. Photography by H.J. Whitlock (ML photograph 1)

Costa's works were written during a fairly fallow period for Festival commissions. However, the Committee, under the guidance of Richard Peyton and later, Robert Harding Milward, were determined to try to attract famous composers to the Festival.

Richard Peyton was a manufacturing chemist and also a member of Birmingham Town Council. He was connected officially with the Triennial Festivals for twenty-four years, variously as orchestral steward, Chairman of the Orchestral Committee, and Chairman of the General Committee. He was very active in persuading the Festival Committee to commission new works from both English and foreign composers. His autograph book (with letters and photographs from many composers and artistes) provides a fascinating record of his activities.[15]

In the mid-1860s, Walter Bache (acting on Peyton's behalf) tried to make contact with Liszt and Wagner. Although neither attempt was successful (Bache had said that he felt *pretty certain in [his] own mind that Wagner would NOT write for any Festival whatsoever*),[16] the Committee was not daunted.

The 1870s saw an increasing number of commissions from composers who were all well-known in their day and indeed from many with international reputations (these were almost always from abroad). The increasing prestige (and, in some cases, substantial fees) attached to such a commission made the Birmingham Festival a magnet for aspiring composers; this letter from Frederic Cowen was fairly typical:

Would you oblige me by laying the enclosed [vocal score] before the Festival Committee at the earliest opportunity and letting me know the result. I am very anxious to write something, no matter what, for the Festival

next year, and perhaps, if the Committee do not meet just yet, you would use your influence for me ...[17]

However, Cowen's vocal score was most unusual in apparently attracting the attention of the Festival Committee as he subsequently won commissions in 1876 (*The Corsair*) and 1885 (*The Sleeping Beauty*).

The works that resulted from the eminent artists that Peyton targeted (and the income they generated) were nearly always worth the efforts of the Committee.

MAX BRUCH

In June 1877 Richard Peyton met Bruch in Cologne and invited him to conduct one of his oratorios at the next Triennial Festival in 1879. Bruch decided this was a good opportunity to compose a new work although this prospect was apparently greeted with less enthusiasm by some of the Festival Committee.

Richard Peyton (taken from Birmingham at the Opening of the Twentieth Century: Contemporary Biographies, ed. WT Pike, 1900)

Peyton wrote to Bruch, evidently airing private and personal concerns relating to the style and content of another choral work, *Frithjof*, written some fifteen years previously. Bruch replied in uncompromising fashion:

Without knowing the musical factions in London, without knowing that the 'Times' reviews are at present written mostly by a red Wagnerian, Mr Hüffer, (who would do better to direct his reproof of 'formlessness' at his Master rather than at me), without, moreover, even taking the trouble to aquaint [sic] yourself with Frithjof, *you rely without further ado on the words of a single newspaper,*

consider Frithjof *a minor and in particular a formless work, which bears a dangerous similarity to 'scrappy music' - and finally, you hope for my own sake that my work for your Festival will not be written in the style of* Frithjof.[18]

Despite this, Bruch was still prepared to bring a new work to Birmingham, although one on a smaller scale than had previously been discussed, because he was too busy elsewhere.

The work that resulted was *The Lay of the Bell (Das Lied von der Glocke)*, based on the poem by Schiller (an allegory illustrating the passage of a human life from birth to death through the processes of casting a bell). It was performed at the 1879 Festival in an English translation by Natalia Macfarren (wife of the composer George) which did less than justice to the original:

Bubbles white the surface cresting,
Lo, the metals glow and fuse,
Caustic alkalis incasting,
Not a virtue shall they lose,
Clear the mass from scum
Pure it must become,
If no flaw or taint be clinging,
Pure and clear shall be its ringing.

The critical response was muted; the Musical Times commented that:

Max Bruch...has endeavoured to give almost a massive grandeur to the choral portions of his work...

and: *On the whole we are inclined to pronounce a favourable verdict upon the Cantata.*[19]

However, the Committee achieved a considerably more positive response with its principal commission for the next Festival.

CHARLES GOUNOD

Gounod was already a very well-known figure in England when he approached the Festival Committee in the late 1870s with the offer to write a work for the next Festival. He said that he would be happy to do this for the outrageous fee of £4,000. It was indicative of Gounod's huge drawing power that a couple of years later (in 1880) the Committee went back to him with an offer of a commission for the 1882 Festival at a fee of £4,000 (Fr 100,000) - an enormous amount of money which they managed to find only by interesting the music publishers Novello in buying the rights for nearly the same amount.

à ma chère amie Georgina Weldon
Ch. Gounod

Charles Gounod

Gounod had a very low opinion of all music publishers and he was particularly unhappy at Novello's potential involvement as it provoked unpleasant memories. Novello had previously been his publisher in England. This relationship started well but soon degenerated into arguments between Gounod and Henry Littleton (of Novello) over royalties. A public airing of Gounod's grievances led to Littleton suing for defamation and costs being awarded against Gounod.

With this in mind, Gounod tried to insist on a number of conditions being agreed before he would accept the new commission:

1) Fr 3,000 paid in costs to Littleton to be returned in full.

2) Fr 100,000 to be paid on delivery of the full score to Novello in settlement of sale and performance rights.

3) Fr 10,000 to be paid by Gounod as potential compensation in case he was unable to direct the first performance in Birmingham.

4) He would retain control of performances in France and Belgium.

5) Performance parts would be produced in numbers according to his specification.[20]

The contract was agreed (although Gounod had to surrender all his rights for his £4,000) and the composer started work on *Redemption*, an oratorio using a text written by him and projected to last three and a half hours.

Gounod had good reason to suspect that there would be problems with his attendance at the performance of *Redemption* in Birmingham because of his infatuation with a married woman several years before.

Georgina Weldon, a singer, had provided a haven for Gounod in 1871 when he avoided the Franco-Prussian war by staying in England. She had apparently no particular romantic motive, preferring instead to mother Gounod and treating him like a spoilt child who was prone to tantrums. She also helped to organise his affairs and bask in his reflected glory. Gounod had adored Mrs Weldon at the outset and promoted her singing career vigorously. However, gradually over the years, he had found her attentiveness restricting and in June 1874 he returned to France and informed her that the relationship was over.

Georgina Weldon 1857 (aged 20)

Mrs Weldon did not consider the matter closed and accused Gounod of living at her expense, virtually rent-free, and as a consequence an acrimonious correspondence was in progress during the time that *Redemption* was being written. Finally, she threatened to serve notice on Gounod as a debtor to her for £2,600 in back rent.

Gounod did conduct the first performance of *Redemption* at the Festival of 1882 where security was very tight. Necessarily so as Mrs Weldon had to be prevented from entering the Town Hall before the performance: an action which made her threaten to sue the entire Festival Committee. She was attempting to gain entrance to leaflet the orchestra and other performers in an effort to obtain publicity for her allegations against Gounod.

Redemption was a huge success and was performed twice, on 30th August and 1st September, to wildly enthusiastic audiences.

The Festival Committee was quite content to indulge Gounod's whims and requests because of his success but this attitude also had the effect of alienating another composer who had been writing a piece for the same Festival.

Julius Benedict was a German emigré who was very well-known in Victorian London as a conductor, composer and impresario. It was at one of his soirées that Gounod first met Georgina Weldon (Benedict was already one of her admirers). His first commission for the Triennial Festival had been in 1870 (the oratorio *St. Peter*) and he was preparing to write a choral work called *Graziella* for the 1882 Festival.

Benedict started to compose the work with specific singers in mind (a common practice) but he soon ran into problems with the Festival Committee. His preferred soprano soloist was needed elsewhere during the Festival and when he wrote to Robert Harding Milward:

Would you kindly inform me whether I may rely upon Mad.e Patey ... Messrs Lloyd and Santley for Alto, Tenor and Baryton [soloists][21]

Robert Harding Milward (taken from Birmingham at the Opening of the Twentieth Century: Contemporary Biographies, ed. WT Pike, 1900)

he was told that Santley would not be available. Understandably he objected to his work being overshadowed and to some extent sidelined by Niels Gade and Gounod and he wrote to Harding Milward:

It will be the first time that I shall not have the pick of the Artistes during the 46 years I have been here.[22]

I have been writing expressly for the Artistes I named in my other letter ... [and] considering that I give my Composition and services for the occasion without asking for any remuneration whatever ...[23]

Benedict felt that the Committee should have been more helpful and their unresolved differences led to the work being abandoned.

The Festival Committee commissioned Gounod again for £4,000 for the next Festival and *Mors et Vita* was another notable success (again being performed twice).

However, this time Georgina Weldon did prevent him from directing the first performance. She had obtained a judgement

against Gounod (while she herself was in prison for slander) totalling £11,640 in damages and costs for alleged debts, breach of contract, defamation, slander and assault. Fortunately the High Court had no jurisdiction in France and Gounod remained there, terrified of being imprisoned (although he vigorously protested his innocence) should he make another appearance in England.

Letter from Gounod to Harding Milward giving the news that Mrs Weldon had won a judgement against him to the tune of £10,000 for a list of alleged offences (Birmingham City Archives, Lee Crowder 1171/76)

16

ANTONIN DVORAK & HANS RICHTER

Dvorak's first commission for the Triennial Festival was performed in 1885, the same year as Gounod's *Mors et Vita*. They were both established, famous composers, yet Dvorak's fee for his work *The Spectre's Bride* was apparently very modest: £200 against Gounod's £4,000.

In fact, Henry Littleton of Novello had taken a considerable risk in offering Gounod the enormous sum of £4,000 for both of his Festival works (a risk that fortunately returned substantial profits) and Dvorak's fee reflected the more usual going rate. Dvorak himself was not convinced and wrote to Littleton in October 1884:

Pray not to pay Mr. Gounod who truly does not need it, so immense sums, for what would be left for me?[24]

Earlier the same year Dvorak had made his first visit to England (at Novello's invitation) to conduct a performance of his *Stabat Mater* at the Royal Albert Hall. It was a notable success and led to Dvorak being in demand by several musical festivals including Birmingham.

The Spectre's Bride was Dvorak's first work to utilise his native folklore although, as was usual in Birmingham, it was sung in an English translation - this time by the Revd Troutbeck (one of Novello's preferred translators) who started by altering the title (*Svatebni Rosile* - literally *The Bridal Shirt*).

Dvorak arrived in Birmingham just prior to the performance and wrote to one of his friends describing the city:

I am here in this immense industrial town where they make excellent knives, scissors, springs, files and I don't know what else, and besides these, music too. And how well. It is terrible what the people here manage to do and to stand! There will be eight concerts in all and each will last four to five hours. My day is Thursday 27th [of August] at 8pm. Please think of me.[25]

The Spectre's Bride was performed to great acclaim and possibly even outshone *Mors et Vita*. Dvorak regarded it as his best work so far and the Sunday Times described it as:

a great and unalloyed success.[26]

The Times wrote:

Herr Dvorak, although he does not possess the graphic power and the orchestral resources of Berlioz or Liszt, has treated a difficult subject with the technical skill and earnest inspiration of a true artist.[27]

The Festival statement of receipts gives some impression of the comparative strengths of each of the main commissions for the 1885 Festival. Gounod's *Mors et Vita* had two performances (following the success of *Redemption*) and attracted a total of 3,387 people; the single performance of Dvorak's *The Spectre's Bride* had an audience of 2,100 - more even than the traditional performance of Mendelssohn's *Elijah*.

The commissions by English composers were much less popular, with Frederic Cowen and Thomas Anderton (a Birmingham resident) only raising an audience of 1,496 between them in two separate concerts. It is interesting to note that although the 1885 Festival was particularly adventurous (containing nine commissions), the total audience was considerably down on previous years at just over 12,000 people and some of the donation of £3,500 to the General Hospital had to be taken out of accumulated funds. The total audience in 1882 had been 13,519 and in 1876 it was 15,016.

Immediately after the première of *The Spectre's Bride*, Harding Milward asked Dvorak for 'a great oratorio' for the 1888 Festival, but the composer stalled in giving an answer, pleading other work. While he was in Birmingham he was given a copy of Newman's *The Dream of Gerontius*, translated into German, as a possible text, but Dvorak eventually declined to set the poem (presumably not finding it suitable).

The Festival Committee persisted and Dvorak gave them the promise of a *Requiem* for the 1891 Festival. He negotiated with Alfred Littleton (Henry's son) at Novello over the fee and in the end agreed to £650, although Novello ignored his request to print the Czech ('Bohemian') version of the title in the vocal score.

After ten months' intensive work, the *Requiem* was completed and given its first performance at Birmingham, conducted by his friend, Hans Richter. Although it made a favourable impression on the audience, the critics' responses were mixed.

Hans Richter had been appointed the Festival's principal conductor in 1885 following the resignation of Michael Costa. Initially his appointment was the cause of some controversy. In particular the composer Arthur Sullivan was quoted as saying:

If it is true that Richter has been, or is to be, offered the Birmingham Festival, I think it is an affront to all of us English. ... I should certainly have considered it an honour if they offered me the festival, whether I could have undertaken it or not. But it is not entirely

selfish, for not a thought of envy or regret should I have felt if Cowen, Stanford, Barnby,

Arthur Sullivan: anonymous cartoon from *The Roundabout*, 2 December 1882

or Randegger (who is one of us to all practical purposes) had been selected. They would have done the work well.[28]

The Festival Committee had been very fortunate in obtaining the services of Richter, who was very active as a conductor both in England and abroad and well-known

Hans Richter outside the Town Hall during the Festival of 1909

for championing new music. He counted several composers, Dvorak and Elgar among them, as personal friends.

Richter oversaw several changes of emphasis in Festival programming; in 1891 an entire morning's concert was taken up by a complete performance of Bach's *St. Matthew Passion* (in English). The scope of the programmes was constantly being stretched, with one concert in 1894 containing works by Cherubini, Wagner (sections of *Parsifal*), Palestrina (*Stabat Mater*), and Mozart. In 1897 the first complete modern performance of the music of Purcell's *King Arthur* was given.

The number of 'Miscellaneous Concerts' was reduced, although the Festival Committee seemed unable to resist the continuing practice of adding extra works at the last minute to a programme that already looked complete: *King Arthur* was performed without an interval, then there was a short break followed by two overtures by Beethoven and Weber, Brahms' *Haydn Variations* and two opera arias.

Although there were new works by British composers during this period (Parry, Stanford, Somervell), none of them had anything like the impact of the principal commission for the first Festival of the new century.

EDWARD ELGAR & THE DREAM OF GERONTIUS

Elgar's first connection with choral festivals as a composer was in 1890 with *Froissart* for the Three Choirs Festival at Worcester. This was also the start of his association with Novello, a connection which was to be very important in the future because of their dominance of British choral music.

In 1896 he wrote his first religious choral work (again for the Three Choirs Festival), *Lux Christi* (*The Light of Life*). The following year saw the start of his friendship with August Jaeger, an editor with Novello - Jaeger had a great belief in Elgar's music and provided very valuable support for a composer bedevilled by depression and lack of self-confidence.

August Jaeger - Elgar's editor and friend

When his oratorio *Caractacus* was performed at the Leeds Festival in 1898 he met Charles Beale of the Birmingham Festival Committee and agreed in principle to write the major commission for the 1900 Triennial Festival.

After deliberation Elgar temporarily abandoned the idea of *The Apostles* due to lack of time, instead he settled on Cardinal Newman's poem *The Dream of Gerontius* for the text for the Festival commission. It had been in the back of his mind for several years, after the poem had been given to him as a wedding present. It also enabled Elgar to use ideas for a 'Gordon' symphony previously promised for, but later retracted from, the Three Choirs Festival (Elgar's copy of *The Dream of Gerontius* was marked with General Gordon's favourite passages).

There was some concern from Elgar about the overtly Catholic content of the poem (although the Festival Committee did not seem worried). On the financial side, there had been previous problems with Novello over the level of royalties and, as a result, his most recent composition, *Sea Pictures*, had been published by Boosey.

On New Year's Day 1900, George Hope Johnstone, Chairman of the Festival Committee, visited Elgar and offered to negotiate with Novello on his behalf.

George Hope Johnstone (taken from Birmingham at the Opening of the Twentieth Century: Contemporary Biographies, ed. WT Pike, 1900)

Johnstone then had a meeting with Alfred Littleton over the terms. Henry Clayton (of Novello) noted:

Agreed this day between Mr. Johnson [sic] of Birmingham and Mr. Alfred H. Littleton to publish Elgar's new Birmingham work The Dream of Gerontius *and to pay Two hundred pounds for all rights. Mr. Johnson undertook to pay £25 for the loan of the necessary vocal & instrumental music for the use of the Festival.[29]*

Johnstone transmitted a crucially different version to Elgar:

They take the whole responsibility of publishing & pay you Two hundred pounds for the work & will, if there is any profit on the sale after the Two Hundred pounds has been cleared, pay you a fair proportion.[30]

Johnstone continued that he hoped that it would not be too long before *Gerontius* reached Novello's but Elgar had nothing ready yet. In fact delays from all quarters were a persistent and, in the end, overwhelming problem.

On 1st March 1900 the first instalment of the composition was sent to Jaeger. By the end of April the first signs of partial chorus scores appeared. However, the initial composition, in the form of a vocal score, was not finished until 1st June.

Elgar wrote:

My work is good to me & I think you will find Gerontius *far beyond anything I've yet done - I LIKE it - I am not suggesting that I have risen to the heights of the poem for one moment but...I've seen in thought the Soul go up & have written my own heart's blood into the score.[31]*

With the Festival only four months away the chorus master, Dr Swinnerton Heap, died suddenly. Immediate problems resulted as there were ten works in preparation. Also the conductor, Hans Richter, could only begin work a few days before the start of the Festival.

Dr Swinnerton Heap had been a great believer in Elgar's music but the Committee had to turn to W.C. Stockley, the retired chorus master, who found himself out of sympathy with the style of the music. Its chromatic nature and continuous form were Wagnerian features foreign to English choral music which had, in general, followed the path set out by Handel's *Messiah,* of separate recitative, aria and chorus. Stockley also objected to the Catholic flavour of the text.

The performance was scheduled for the beginning of October but by the start of June chorus parts had still not been prepared and were not expected until July. In fact they finally arrived in the middle of August. More problems were caused by there being only one full score to be passed in sections around all the people who needed it ie. Elgar, Jaeger, William Dodd (Novello's copyist), and the engravers.

A note from Dodd dated 18th August gives some impression of the problems:

Mr. Elgar had already told me about Richter wanting score, & am working with that object. I think I shall be sure to finish with it by the time that he wants it. I am unable to give a date as the score is so very complicated. I will send you part of the score in a day or two.[32]

Telegram from Elgar to Jaeger dated 18th September 1900 giving some idea of the frantic preparations to get the orchestral material ready for the first performance of *The Dream of Gerontius* (Birmingham City Archives MS2067)

The chorus had considerable problems due to the limited number of rehearsals available and the complexity of Elgar's writing. The orchestral parts were still not available, with work continuing at a frantic pace throughout September.

Richter had first sight of the full score only ten days before the first performance and managed only one separate orchestral rehearsal. At the first and only scheduled complete rehearsal on Saturday, 29th September 1900, Elgar was present as were a large number of spectators.

There were considerable problems at the rehearsal and this lead to an intervention by Elgar. The Sheffield Independent reported:

Having tolerated much, he suddenly left his seat in the hall, hurried to the orchestra, and stopped the chorus, declaring the rhythm was wrong, the time wrong, and all unsatisfactory. 'There is', he exclaimed, 'no accent. It is nothing. The whole colour is gone. It is like a ballad in a drawing room.' [33]

The rehearsal was curtailed and although an extra chorus rehearsal was arranged, the omens were not good.

The first performance on 3rd October was a disaster. A friend of Elgar's noted:

Letter from Johnstone to Alfred Littleton written after the disastrous first performance of *The Dream of Gerontius* in which Johnstone refers to Novello's description of the work as 'a financial failure' (Birmingham City Archives MS2067)

Before the end of the Kyrie it was evident that the Chorus did not know the parts they were trying to sing, and as the music became more chromatic they slipped hideously out of tune. [Part II was] hopelessly wrecked by the choir, whose pitiful stumblings indeed remained the outstanding impression...The whole thing was a nightmare.[34]

However, the work, if not the performance, was strongly applauded and the critics also looked beyond the travesty of the performance and were mostly very impressed

The Musical Standard stated:

It is music which could not have been written by any man who had not felt the beauty of Newman's Angel...[35]

The London Musical Courier reported that:

For the first time in history, it seems to me, a provincial festival commission has been successful in bringing to birth a choral work by an Englishman worthy in any way of arrogating to itself the title 'a great art work' ... I, for one, felt all my preconceived antagonism to the poem melt away before Elgar's setting, and left the hall throbbing with emotion that no English work has raised in me heretofore.[36]

Despite this, Elgar felt acutely depressed and the dispute with Novello over royalties flared again. He received a cheque for £200 as full and final payment and when he queried the possibility of royalties, Johnstone came to his rescue. A correspondence between Littleton and Johnstone followed. Novello regarded *The Dream of Gerontius* as a total commercial failure and, as they had no expectation of recouping the fee paid to Elgar, any question of royalties was not to be discussed. Johnstone was not deterred and finally got Littleton to agree to pay a royalty in the unlikely event of the work making money.

Johnstone demonstrated his unwavering faith in Elgar's work in a letter to Littleton:

Please accept my warmest thanks for your generosity in reference to Elgar's work: it is very kind & I appreciate it very much: I hope for Elgar's sake that he may some day reap the benefit of his great work, for it is one of the greatest works ever written by an Englishman & I hope some day it may have full justice done to it which it did not at the Festival, solely owing to insufficient rehearsals. I trust some good Chorus may render it in a way that will make it popular & that you may ultimately reap the reward of your enterprise.[37]

He did not have to wait very long: a friend of Jaeger's, Professor Julius Buths from Dusseldorf, had been at the first performance and, undaunted, gave another performance in Dusseldorf in December 1901 - this was a great and unqualified success which drew a considerable compliment from Richard Strauss who proposed a toast to *the welfare and success of the first English progressivist, Meister Edward Elgar.*[38]

Elgar himself wrote to Novello:

Will you accept my heartiest thanks for all your kindness in furthering the performance of Gerontius here: I am most grateful & am glad that the work was in every way successful. ... As to the performance; it completely bore out my own idea of the work: the Chorus was very fine and had only commenced work on Nov. 11 - this disproves the idea fostered in Birmingham that my work is too difficult.[39]

Such acknowledgement abroad made English festivals reconsider the work, which rapidly became in demand, and also encouraged Elgar to return to large-scale works for choir.

THE APOSTLES

After the later much-improved reception of *Gerontius*, the Festival Committee asked Elgar for another commission for the 1903 Festival. Elgar returned to the idea of *The Apostles* on a grand scale.

The story of *The Apostles* was Christian without being identified with either the Catholic or Protestant Churches. Elgar saw

it as a Christian allegory of a creative life - he identified with this and with a picture of *Christ in the Wilderness* which hung in his study. Additionally, the recent death of his mother led him to think deeply about his religious beliefs.

He asked Edward Capel-Cure (the librettist of *Lux Christi*) to give advice on the libretto, which Elgar wanted to grow together with the music. He wrote to Ivor Atkins:

I am now plotting GIGANTIC WORX.[40]

Johnstone again acted on his behalf with the publishers; Elgar had left Novello again for Boosey, and Johnstone was able to play them off against each other. He started by

Letter from Johnstone to Littleton discussing terms for Elgar's latest Birmingham commission *The Apostles* (Birmingham City Archives MS2067)

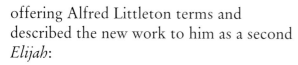

offering Alfred Littleton terms and described the new work to him as a second *Elijah*:

I am very anxious to do all I can for Elgar, and my proposition is that you should buy the work for a Thousand pounds with a small royalty on each copy sold, & I feel convinced that it will be a most profitable speculation.[41]

Littleton did not agree and wanted to see some of the music (as did Boosey) but Elgar could only supply the following outline of a proposed trilogy of separate works:

I   The schooling [of the Apostles].
II   The earthly result.
III The result of it all in the next world...Last Judgement & the next world as in Revelations.

Negotiations with Novello continued, with Johnstone offering £500 on completion, the other £500 after 10,000 copies had been sold, and a royalty thereafter. But the lack of a fixed libretto to show any prospective publisher caused problems although composition was under way.

As this was towards the end of 1902 and less than a year from the first performance, Elgar realised he would have to focus exclusively on the first work - itself to be in three sections.

By the end of March 1903, he was only halfway through Part 1 of *The Apostles*, which was already over an hour's music. By the beginning of May only half the entire work was completed and there was not even a libretto for the remainder. At this point Elgar decided to shorten the third part considerably.

By the end of June, Part 2 was nearly complete but Elgar had started to have second thoughts about some of the earlier

material. Jaeger was very worried about production of the choral parts given the previous disaster and he wrote to Elgar urging him to leave the completed sections as they were so that they could be printed off by Novello.

Elgar was suffering problems with his eyesight and realised that Part 3 was not going to be possible. He sent his wife, Alice, to Birmingham to get Johnstone's agreement to perform the work in its truncated form. Elgar wrote to Novello with the result:

I was not able to get to Birmingham to-day but Mrs. Elgar went and saw Mr Johnstone: they - or rather he is quite satisfied to produce Pts I & II & thinks it best to say nothing of any change of plan.[42]

At this point Elgar abandoned the third part entirely and drew a line under the rest of the composition. This allowed rehearsals to start on Part 1 at the beginning of July under a new chorus master.

Elgar himself was to conduct the first performance and the final rehearsals went well. On 14th October the Town Hall was packed; the Birmingham Daily Mail reported:

When Dr. Elgar took his seat shortly before half-past eleven every inch of the interior of the vast building was occupied by an audience which will undoubtedly rank as one of the most brilliant of the many distinguished companies seen within the walls of the historic hall. A conspicuous figure in the front row of the great gallery was Madam Clara Butt, who had as her companion Mrs Elgar.[43]

Alice Elgar wrote:

Wonderful performance & wonderful impression on audience, the quiet & silence at end of 1st part, the highest tribute. Last chorus overwhelming.[44]

It was a triumphant success; the Worcester Herald wrote:

At the conclusion of the work the audience remained unwilling to mar the devotional effect of such a masterpiece by applause. It was, however, only for a few moments, and then the enthusiasm was not to be restrained...[45]

Johnstone wrote to Littleton after the performance:

I trust that you are thoroughly satisfied with the results of the first performance of The Apostles *which was so successfully produced at the Festival. As you are aware the applications for tickets were 700 or 800 more than we could possibly accommodate and I am convinced that its success as a musical work is assured.*[46]

Elgar was now acknowledged as a major composer and a famous public figure - a position consolidated with his knighthood the following year.

THE KINGDOM

In November 1904 Elgar was appointed Peyton Professor of Music at Birmingham University - a post which had been created specially for him. Although this was a great honour for him, it did involve preparing and giving public lectures, which had considerable implications for his composing. He was also principal conductor of the recently-formed London Symphony Orchestra.

He gave a series of lectures in 1905 as part of his teaching duties. One lecture in particular: 'A Future for English Music' caused considerable public comment because of its criticism of the musical establishment. This affected Elgar who was trying to start work on the sequel to *The Apostles* (Part II of the grand plan) which had been

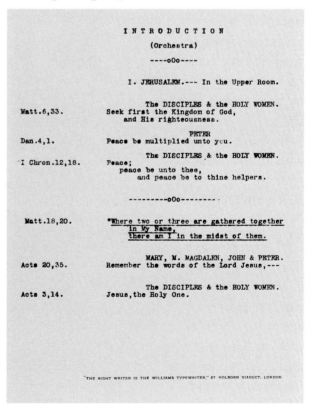

Typescript of the libretto for *The Kingdom* giving the Biblical sources for the text (Birmingham City Archives MS2067)

commissioned by the Triennial Festival Committee for the 1906 Festival.

At the beginning of 1906, Elgar wrote to Novello:

By this post I send the first scrap of the new work - title to be considered: it should be "The Kingdom of God".

This portion is only the introduction but the rest should follow soon: this portion must of course end a page.[47]

In fact, the rest did not follow easily. Elgar was often unwell and a planned trip to America in April and May precluded the possibility of any composition for this period.

In February, Elgar was ready to resign from the entire Birmingham commission. Alice Elgar talked to Alfred Littleton about the possibility of the Triennial Festival accepting, in effect, only half the projected work in order to relieve the overwhelming pressure on the composer. This was agreed by the Festival Committee. Elgar continued the struggle and by the end of March about half of the shortened version was ready. The interruption caused by the American tour and the news of his father's recent death affected Elgar badly. By June Novello's were worrying about the printing. Elgar wrote to Littleton:

This illness had quite upset my plans for everything. I now see my way D.V. to let you have the final M.S. of this portion in July. You can print in August & the Chorus can quite well learn the remainder in September: so all will be well. I very much regret causing any inconvenience but I find I cannot 'work up' my sketches when I'm ill.[48]

Both *The Apostles* and *The Kingdom* were performed at the 1906 Triennial Festival with Elgar conducting. The first performance of *The Kingdom* moved him deeply. The Birmingham Mail observed:

Sir Edward Elgar's emotions were so stirred by his own wonderful work that, according to the observation of the choristers, tears were streaming down his face several times during the oratorio.[49]

The press response was very mixed; Ernest Newman in the [Birmingham] Daily Post wrote:

The general level of inspiration is, in my opinion, below that of Gerontius *or* The Apostles. *Some of the choral portions are so obvious in sentiment that one can hardly believe they came from the delicately spiritual brain that conceived* Gerontius *... A great deal of the music must frankly be called dull in itself ...*[50]

Sir Edward Elgar O.M.

Elgar, as usual, was very depressed after the first performance and resolved never to start work on the third and final section of the full work - *The Last Judgement*.

THE MUSIC MAKERS

In 1911 Elgar continued to suffer from problems with his health and he was depressed over the comparative failure of his second symphony which was held to be out of sympathy with the audience's expectations. At this time he also severed his long-term connection with Novello, leaving his compositions to survive in the marketplace.

His fourth and final commission for the Triennial Festival was *The Music Makers*. Elgar chose to use O'Shaughnessy's *Ode* which he decided reflected in many ways his current feelings and emotions:

The mainspring of O'Shaughnessy's Ode *is the sense of progress, of never-ceasing challenge; it is the duty of the artist to see that this inevitable change is progress. With a deep sense of this trust, I have endeavoured to interpret the* Ode *as shewing the continuity of art in spite of those dreamers and singers who dream and sing "no more".*

In interpreting [his] ode, I have felt that his "music makers" must include not only poets and singers but all artists who feel the tremendous responsibility of their mission to "renew the world of yore". As I have felt, so I have insisted on this responsibility, therefore the atmosphere of the music is mainly sad; but there are moments of enthusiasm, and bursts of joy occasionally approaching frenzy; moods which the creative artist suffers in creating or in contemplation of the unending influence of his creation.[51]

Elgar decided to set the entire poem without alteration and, as he saw it as a self-portrait

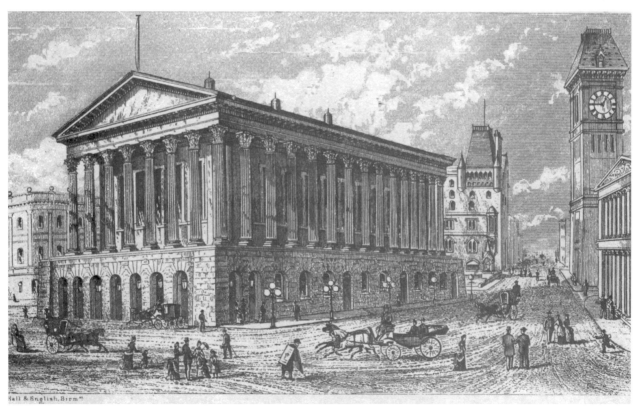

Engraving showing the Town Hall at the end of the nineteenth century

The closing bars of *The Music Makers*

to a large extent, *The Music Makers* was to have significant and extensive allusions to his earlier compositions. These were used with apparent feelings of wistful remembrance.

The most obvious source of music was from *The Enigma Variations* where the two main elements of the theme were closely shadowed in the main themes for *The Music Makers*.

Elgar wrote:

I have used the opening bars of the theme (Enigma) of the variations because it expressed when written (in 1898) my sense of the loneliness of the artist as described in the first six lines of the Ode, *and to me, it still embodies that sense...*[52]

Later in the work Elgar re-used the entire *Nimrod* theme set for solo alto as a tribute to Jaeger. Material from the first symphony, *The Dream of Gerontius*, violin concerto and *The Apostles* all found a place within the new work.

The new work was thus intensely personal and retrospective, with the flavour of an

English oratorio composed during the previous century. When it was performed at the Triennial Festival in 1912 (in the same programme as Sibelius' fourth symphony) the response was not enthusiastic.
One paper said:

Where The Music Makers *falls short is in the unreality of the theme. ... did a single member of the chorus who sang those words, or one person in to-night's audience, really believe them? ... Music set to this ode could not therefore be expected to have great strength or sincerity.*[53]

The correspondent of the Daily Telegraph commented:

I do not find on one hearing of The Music Makers *that its note is so much of sadness as of unsatisfied yearning. ... The music is often of exquisite beauty, but ... its very mood is against it - this mood of yearning, alternating with a confident mood of massive power, and finally bringing a return to the prevailing lack of confidence, as if the subject were greater than the composer could translate into terms of music.*[54]

This was Elgar's last major choral work.

EPILOGUE

The Triennial Festival of 1912 (with Sir Henry Wood as principal conductor) contained five commissions or first performances within the four days that it lasted and the Festival programme book gave the outward impression of a continuing success.

However, a comparison between the balance sheets of the Festivals of 1900 and 1912 gives a very different picture.

In 1900 the total attendance was 13,333 people who generated receipts of £15,282, allowing approximately £4,000 to be donated to the General Hospital. This was not that much when compared to earlier Festivals when the same amount was donated from a much smaller turnover.

In 1912 the total attendance was only 8,702 and so the Festival's receipts were substantially less at £10,831. The lack of income was compounded by the expenses of a high-profile programme which totalled £9,282. Such money as was left went towards an operating deficit from the 1909 and 1912 Festivals which totalled more than £2,000: no money at all went to the General Hospital.

The Great War intervened, breaking the sequence of Festivals which was never resumed; the social and musical fabric of the city moved away from the format and thinking behind the Triennial Festivals.

This was the end of a glorious period in Birmingham's cultural history during which *choral works had frequently been in the van of progress. It had been an era of magnificent toil, strife, and struggle, and it culminated with the promise that a truly self-sufficient national art would, at last, be born.*[55]

A reply to an over-zealous librarian confirming the demise of the Triennial Festivals

Walter Powell Esq.,
Central Libraries,
Ratcliffe Place,
BIRMINGHAM.

J. E. PRITCHARD, SHERWOOD & Co.
~~J. E. PRITCHARD & Co.~~
CHARTERED ACCOUNTANTS.
TELEPHONE: CENTRAL 1476.
TELEGRAMS
COLLOCATE, BIRMINGHAM.
J.E.PRITCHARD.
H. H. SHERWOOD.

REC'D OCT. 1st

Kings Court.
115, Colmore Row.
Birmingham.

30th September 1920.

Dear Sir,

Replying to your application of the 16th inst for copies of programmes of the Triennial Musical Festival. A Festival has not been held since 1912, a copy of the programme of which was sent to you, and the promotion of a Festival on similar lines is very improbable.

Yours faithfully,

30

REFERENCES

1. The Birmingham Central Library currently has lists of the BFCS archive holdings. This material will be transferred gradually to the City Archives section of the library.

2. For more detailed information on the early years of the Festival see TIBBLES, A.J. The rise of the Birmingham Musical Festivals, 1768-1834 BA dissertation, 1970

3. BUNCE, J.T. [History of the Birmingham Musical Festival 1768-1870] newspaper article mounted in book form, 1873. p.40

4. Quoted ibid., p.40

5. Quoted in EDWARDS, F.G. The history of Mendelssohn's oratorio "Elijah" Novello, Ewer & Co., 1896. p.29

6. Letter of 11.12.1845 Birmingham City Archives MS 1292/5/3

7. Letter of 8.5.1846 Birmingham City Archives, MS 1292/5/5

8. Letter of 26.8.1846 quoted in EDWARDS, F.G. op. cit., p.85-6

9. Birmingham City Archives, MS 1292/5/6

10. 29.8.1846 quoted in EDWARDS, F.G. op. cit., p.96

11. MASON, L. Musical letters from abroad New York, 1854. p.196-7

12. ibid., p.209

13. ibid., p.203

14. BURTON, N. 'Oratorios and cantatas' in The romantic age 1800-1914 Athlone Press, 1981. p.226

15. PEYTON, R. [Autograph book] Birmingham City Archives, MS 1552/1

16. Undated letter to Peyton Birmingham City Archives, MS 1552/1/33

17. Letter of 17.7.1872 to Peyton Birmingham City Archives, MS 1552/1/85

18. Translation of a letter of 26.6.1878 Birmingham City Archives, MS 1596/1

19. 1.10.1879 quoted in FIFIELD, C. Max Bruch: his life and works Gollancz, 1988. p.163

20. Translation and paraphrase of a letter from Gounod to Robert Harding Milward in 1880 prior to the official agreement Birmingham City Archives, Lee Crowder 1171/54

21. Letter of 31.1.1882 Birmingham City Archives, Lee Crowder 1171/9

22. Letter of 4.2.1882 Birmingham City Archives, Lee Crowder 1171/10

23. Letter of 22.2.1882 Birmingham City Archives, Lee Crowder 1171/11

24. Letter reproduced in ROBERTSON, A. Dvorak Dent, 1974. after p.82

25. Letter to Alois Gobl (date not given) quoted in BUTTERWORTH, N. Dvorak: his life and times Midas Books, 1980. p.60

26. 30.8.1885

27. 28.8.1885

28. Quoted in NETTEL, R. The orchestra in England Jonathan Cape, 1947. p.223

29. Note dated 23.1.1900 Birmingham City Archives, MS 2067

30. Letter of 30.1.1900 ibid.

31. Letter of 27.6.1900 to Nicholas Kilburn quoted in MOORE, J.N. Edward Elgar: a creative life Oxford University Press, 1984. p.315

32. Note to Novello Birmingham City Archives, MS 2067

33. 8.10.1900 quoted in MOORE, J.N. op. cit., p.329

34. BURLEY, R. & CARRUTHERS, F. Edward Elgar: the record of a friendship Barrie & Jenkins, 1972. p.142

35. Edward Baughan in the issue of 6.10.1900 quoted in MOORE, J.N. op. cit., p.332

36. 12.10.1900 quoted ibid., p.333

37. Letter of 22.11.1900 Birmingham City Archives, MS 2067

38. Quoted in KENNEDY, M. Portrait of Elgar 3rd ed. Oxford University Press, 1987. p.129

39. Letter of 21.12.1901 Birmingham City Archives, MS 2067

40. Letter of 2.7.1902 quoted in MOORE, J.N. op. cit., p.372

41. Letter of 3.7.1902 Birmingham City Archives, MS 2067

42. Letter of 29.6.1903 to Henry Clayton ibid.

43. 15.10.1903 quoted in MOORE, J.N. op. cit., p.415

44. Quoted ibid., p.415

45. 17.10.1903 quoted ibid., p.416

46. Letter of 20.10.1903 Birmingham City Archives, MS 2067

47. Letter of 4.1.1906 to Littleton ibid.

48. Letter of 25.6.1906 quoted in MOORE, J.N. op. cit., p.500

49. 4.10.1906 quoted ibid., p.505

50. 4.10.1906 quoted ibid., p.506

51. 'Introductory note' to 'The Music Makers' sent 14.8.1912 to Ernest Newman quoted ibid., p.631-2

52. Ibid. quoted ibid., p.633

53. Cutting from unidentified newspaper quoted ibid., p.639

54. Robin Legge in the issue of 2.10.1912 quoted ibid., p.639

55. BURTON, N. op. cit., p.241

APPENDIX I

FIRST PERFORMANCES AS PART OF THE BIRMINGHAM TRIENNIAL MUSIC FESTIVALS

Sigismund Neukomm	David	1834
Felix Mendelssohn	Piano concerto no. 2	1837
Felix Mendelssohn	Lobgesang (first UK)	1840
Felix Mendelssohn	Elijah	1846
Felix Mendelssohn	A Saviour of Sinners– Ave Maria op.23 no.2 (first UK)	1852
Felix Mendelssohn	Christus (first UK)	1852
Felix Mendelssohn	Lorelei	1852
S. S. Wesley	The Wilderness	1852
Michael Costa	Eli	1855
Henry Leslie	Judith	1858
Michael Costa	Naaman	1864
Henry Smart	The Bride of Dunkerron	1864
Arthur Sullivan	Kenilworth	1864
Julius Benedict	When My Thirsty Soul (song)	1867
John Francis Barnett	The Ancient Mariner	1867
W. Sterndale Bennett	The Woman of Samaria	1867
John Francis Barnett	Paradise and the Peri	1870
Julius Benedict	St. Peter	1870
Ferdinand Hiller	Nala and Demayanti	1870
Robert P. Stewart	Ode to Shakespeare	1870
Arthur Sullivan	Overture Di Ballo	1870
Alberto Randegger	Fridolin	1873
Gioacchino Rossini	Hymn of Peace (first UK)	1873
Gioacchino Rossini	The Song of the Titans (first UK)	1873
Gioacchino Rossini	Ave Maria	1873
Gioacchino Rossini	Cantemus	1873
Francesco Schira	Lord Burleigh	1873
Arthur Sullivan	Light of the World	1873
Frederic H. Cowen	The Corsair	1876
Niels Gade	Zion	1876
George Macfarren	The Resurrection	1876
Richard Wagner	Liebesmahl des Apostel (first UK)	1876
Max Bruch	The Lay of the Bell	1879
Camille Saint-Saens	La Lyre et la Harpe	1879
Niels Gade	Psyche	1882
Alfred Gaul	The Holy City	1882

Charles Gounod	Redemption	1882
Charles Gounod	The Golden Thread (song)	1882
Charles Gounod	Wedding March no.2	1882
Thomas Anderton	Yule Tide	1885
J. Frederick Bridge (Latin version by Gladstone of 'Rock of Ages')	Jesus, pro me	1885
Frederic H. Cowen	Sleeping Beauty	1885
Antonin Dvorak	The Spectre's Bride	1885
Charles Gounod	Mors et Vita	1885
Alexander Mackenzie	Invocation: scena– 'Love lost on earth'	1885
Alexander Mackenzie	Violin concerto	1885
Ebenezer Prout	Symphony no. 3	1885
Charles V. Stanford	Three Holy Children	1885
J. Frederick Bridge	Callirhoe	1888
Edvard Grieg	In Autumn (first performance of the orchestral version)	1888
C. Hubert Parry	Judith	1888
Antonin Dvorak	Requiem	1891
Alexander Mackenzie	Veni Creator Spiritus	1891
Charles V. Stanford	Eden	1891
Goring Thomas	The Dawn	1891
George Henschel	Stabat Mater	1894
C. Hubert Parry	King Saul	1894
Goring Thomas	The Swan & the Skylark	1894
Edward German	Hamlet (Symphonic poem)	1897
Arthur Somervell	An Ode to the Sea	1897
Charles V. Stanford	Requiem	1897
Edward Elgar	Dream of Gerontius	1900
C. Hubert Parry	The Soldier's Tent (song)	1900
Anton Bruckner	Te Deum (first UK)	1903
Edward Elgar	The Apostles	1903
Granville Bantock	Omar Khayyam Pt 1&2	1906
Edward Elgar	The Kingdom	1906
Joseph Holbrooke	The Bells	1906
Percy Pitt	Sinfonietta in G min	1906
Christian Ritter	Amantissime sponse Jesu (first UK)	1906
Granville Bantock	Omar Khayyam Pt 3	1909
Rutland Boughton	Midnight (Symphonic poem, with chorus)	1909
Granville Bantock	Fifine at the Fair	1912
Edward Elgar	The Music Makers	1912
Alexander Scriabin	Prometheus (first UK)	1912
Jean Sibelius	Symphony no. 4 (first UK)	1912
Walford Davies	Song of St. Francis	1912

APPENDIX II

GEORGE BERNARD SHAW AND THE BIRMINGHAM FESTIVALS

Bernard Shaw was:

One of the most brilliant critics, not only of the drama, but also of music, who have ever worked in London, or indeed anywhere.

Grove's Dictionary of Music 1954

For six years as a regular columnist and thereafter sporadically, and sometimes anonymously, Shaw's great qualities of common sense and humour enlivened the breakfast tables of music lovers everywhere.

As Hesketh Pearson put it:

He wrote in order to be read by people who did not know a crotchet from a quaver; and for the first and only time in British criticism, the man in the street could enjoy a column of journalism devoted to music. In a country where solemnity passes for profundity and irreverence for superficiality, it was naturally assumed that he did not know what he was writing about.

Actually he knew quite as much about it as any of the academic folk who were scandalized because the layman had been made to laugh: and it is pleasant to record that while the Parrys, Stanfords, Mackenzies and other musical bigwigs of that time were holding up their hands in shocked amazement, the greatest of English composers, Edward Elgar, then a young and struggling teacher of music , was enjoying Shaw's quips so heartily that when they met one another in late life the composer was able to quote many passages which the critic had long forgotten.

Hesketh Pearson. Bernard Shaw: a biography. Methuen 1961

The following examples of his music criticism in which he turned upon the spectacle of the English musical world of the day an eye unclouded by tradition, a judgement unaffected by social or official considerations (Ernest Newman in his Sunday Times review of 'Music in London' of 1932), are taken from The Bodley Head Bernard Shaw: Shaw's Music edited by Dan. H. Laurence.1981 by kind permission of The Society of Authors on behalf of the Bernard Shaw Estate.

THE BIRMINGHAM FESTIVAL

I cannot say that I am unmixedly grateful to the Birmingham Festival people. They brought me all the way from Venice by a polite assurance that a packet of tickets awaited my arrival. But when, after a headlong rush over the Alps and far away into the Midlands, I reached the Town Hall, insufferable indignities were put upon me. The stewards on the floor declared that my seat was in the gallery; the stewards in the gallery insisted that it was on the floor; and finally, when it became plain that no seat at all had been reserved, I was thrust ignominiously into a corner in company with a couple of draughts and an echo, and left to brood vengefully over the performance. On the Passion Music day I escaped the corner, and shared a knifeboard at the back of the gallery with a steward who kept Bach off by reading the Birmingham Daily Post, and breathed so hard when he came to the bankruptcy list that it was plain that every firm mentioned in it was heavily in his debt.

Under these circumstances, no right-minded person will grudge a certain vindictive satisfaction in recording that the performance of the St. Matthew Passion, which was what I came from Venice to hear, was not, on the whole, a success.

From The World 14 October 1891

GOUNOD'S REDEMPTION

M. Gounod is almost as hard to dispraise as the President of the Royal Academy. Both produce works so graceful, so harmonious, so smooth, so delicate, so refined, and so handsomely sentimental, that it is difficult to convey, without appearing ungracious or insensible, the exact measure of disparagement needed to prevent the reader from concluding that M. Gounod is another Handel. And indeed M. Gounod does not express his ideas worse than Handel; but then he has fewer ideas to express. No one has ever been bored by an adequate performance of the Messiah...But the best conceivable performance of the Redemption would not hold an audience to the last note if the half-past-five train back to town from Sydenham were at stake, much less make them impatient for a repetition of the oratorio, which is, in truth, an extremely tedious work, not because any particular number is dull or repulsive, but because its beauties are repeated ad nauseam.

From The Dramatic Review, 8 May 1886

GOUNOD'S MORS ET VITA

M. Gounod's oratorio is dedicated to Pope Leo XIII. The descriptions at hand do not represent it as a cheerful work. It begins with a Requiem. Judgement follows Death; but the upshot is happy, as Judgement leads to Life. This is a large order for M. Gounod. Exquisite as he always was in his sentiment, and graceful as he is in his piety, he is hardly the man to take the field with Bach and Handel, who were as much more modest in choosing their subjects as they were more powerful in handling them.

About the religious music of the XIX century there is a desperate triviality which shews how far human seriousness has been divorced from the legendary externals of our creeds. Our really serious music is no longer recognized as religious, whilst our professedly religious music, though laboriously composed in the "impressive" style, is no more serious than the third act of Robert le Diable. We have already had from M. Gounod the Redemption musically illustrated by a March to Calvary with orchestral effects. And now we have the resurrection depicted by tremolando passages and more "effects" for six trumpets. Religious music of this sort is only remarkable as naive blasphemy, wonderfully elaborated, and convinced of its own piety. Doubtless, many of the public are pleased, much as they would be if, on going to church, they found sensational novels bound up in their Bible covers, and were surprised to find Scripture so amusing.

From unsigned notes in The Dramatic Review, 29 August 1885

GOUNOD'S MORS ET VITA

M. Gounod is no Voltairean: he is the romantically pious Frenchman whose adoration of the Virgin Mary is chivalrous, whose obedience to the Pope is filial, and whose homage to his God is that of a devoted royalist to his king. It follows that he is not a deep thinker. But his exquisite taste, his fastidious workmanship, and an earnestness that never fails him even in his most childish enterprises, makes him the most enchanting of modern musicians within the limits of his domain of emotion and picturesque superstition.

From 'Our Corner' December 1885

GOUNOD'S MORS ET VITA

A performance that begins at half-past-seven and is not over until twenty minutes to eleven would make most audiences restive, even if the composer were at liberty to range from grave to gay, from lively to severe, as at the opera. In an oratorio this is of course out of the question; and in Mors et Vita there are hardly any of those exciting mundane incidents which help the British public through the popular works of Handel and Mendelssohn. Mors et Vita will be described by many honest Philistines as being as long as an oratorio and as dull as a Mass. The ideas dealt with are nearly all subjective: there is no stoning of Saints, leaping upon altars, fiery chariots, or suggested spectacular melodrama of any sort; nor is there anything parallel to the raging mob in the St. Matthew Passion, or the chorus of scoffers in the Messiah...

In fact, much of Mors et Vita may be described as a mystery with modern ballet music. Audiences are growing accustomed to this.
Since the Almighty was brought upon the stage in Boito's Mefistofele, speaking, or rather singing, through the mouths of the chorus, we seem to have become hardened to piously-intended blasphemy. The Supreme Judge has a good deal to say in the third part of Mors et Vita, and he says it with dignity and refinement, quite en grand seigneur, being apparently conceived by M. Gounod on the lines of that noble gentleman, Athos in Les Trois Mousquetaires.

From unsigned notes in The Dramatic Review, 7 November 1885

PARRY; JUDITH

The truth about the oratorio is one of those matters which a critic is sorely tempted to mince. Mr Parry is a gentleman of culture and independent means, pursuing his beloved art with a devotion and disinterestedness which is not possible to musicians who have to live by their profession. He is guiltless of potboilers and catchpennies, and both in his compositions and in his excellent literary essays on music, he has proved the constant elevation of his musical ideal. Never was there a musician easier and pleasanter to praise, painfuller and more ungracious to disparage, But-! yes, there is a serious but in the case on the present occasion; and its significance is that when a man takes it upon himself to write an oratorio - perhaps the most gratuitous exploit open to a XIX century Englishman - he must take the consequences.

Judith, then, consists of a sort of musical fabric that any gentleman of Mr Parry's general culture, with a turn for music and the requisite technical training, can turn out to any extent needful for the purposes of a Festival Committee. There is not a rhythm in it, not a progression, not a modulation that brings a breath of freshness with it...Madame Patey as Meshullemeth discoursed in lugubrious dramatic recitative about desolate courts and profaned altars. She was repaid for her thankless exertions by one popular number in the form of a ballad which consisted of the first line of The Minstrel Boy, followed by the second line of Tom Bowling, connected by an "augmentation" of a passage from the finale of the second act of Lucrezia Borgia, with an ingenious blend of The Girl I Left Behind Me and We be Three Poor Mariners.

From The Star, 18 December 1888; signed "By 'The Star's' Own Captious Critic"

Novello & Company played a pivotal role in the development of choral music in England.

Founded by Vincent Novello at the beginning of the century, the business was established as a full commercial enterprise by his eldest son, J. Alfred Novello, who soon discovered the artistic and commercial possibilities of cheap editions of standard works. The firm both fostered and catered for the growth of interest in choral music through its comparatively cheap 'Octavo editions', initially published in 'The Musical Times', which it founded in 1844.

NOVELLO

No human being ever liked a Church Cantata written to order for one of our provincial Festivals. Here it is, in the familiar Novello buff and brown cover, price two shillings. The words, I blush to say, are by a brother critic. Listen!

Rest thee, my Savior, rest Thy head meetly.
Angels watch over Thee sleeping so sweetly.
No dream alarm
with thought of harm
Til night and its shadows have vanished completely.

Take it away, Messrs Novello, take it away. Burn the whole edition, lest any choral society should waste its time on rhyme-jingling that never once rises to the level of blasphemy, and on music-mongering that is enough to make every intelligent student in England forswear counterpoint. I suppose the stewards of the.....Musical festival thought they were encouraging English music by ordering a cantata; and I am bound to assume that my colleague of the largest circulation in the world is honestly and infatuatedly unconscious of how detestable his verses are from a literary point of view... but there are limits to the allowances I am prepared to make. In future it will be necessary to square The Star if the truth about these matters is to remain untold any longer. Either I must have my share of the libretto-making or I blow the gaff.

From 'A Portfolio of New Music' The Star, 1 November 1889

DVORAK'S REQUIEM

Dvorak's Requiem bored Birmingham so desperately that it was unanimously voted a work of extra-ordinary depth and impressiveness, which verdict I record with a hollow laugh, and allow the subject to drop by its own portentous weight. Besides, I do not wish to belie that steward who introduced me to his colleague on Thursday morning (when I was looking for a seat) as "one of these complimentary people."

From The World 14 October 1891

I gave Dvorak's requiem one more chance on Wednesday last, when it was performed - and very well performed too - for the first time in London, at the Albert Hall, under Mr Barnby. And I am more amazed than ever that any critic should mistake this paltry piece of orchestral and harmonic confectionery for a serious composition.

From The World 30 March 1892

To Dvorak's Requiem, which was performed last Wednesday at the Albert Hall, I could not be made to listen again, since the penalty of default did not exceed death; and I had much rather die than repeat the attempts I made, first at Birmingham, and then at Kensington Gore, to sit it out... the public, in spite of Charles Dickens, loves everything connected with a funeral. Those who are too respectable to stand watching the black flag after an execution take a creepy sort of pleasure in Requiems. If Sir Joseph Barnby were to conduct with a black brass-tipped baton; if the bandsmen wore black gloves and crape scarves; if the attendants were professional mutes (sordini) and the tickets edged with a half-inch jet border, I believe the enjoyment of the audience would be immensely enhanced.

...a funeral goes past in less than two minutes, whereas a Requiem takes a matter of two hours. Besides, it is generally understood that funerals are to be avoided as long as possible, whereas Requiems are offered as a sort of treat, whether anybody is dead or not.

From The World 9 November 1892

ELGAR: THE APOSTLES

The Apostles is one of the glories of British music: indeed it is unique as a British work. Its quality is such that German music at its highest in this form can put nothing beside it except the St Matthew Passion of Bach, a few samples from the Messiah of what Handel could have done with the same theme, and Beethoven's great Mass in D.

It places British music once more definitely in the first European rank, after two centuries of leather and prunella.

From a letter to The Daily News, London, 9 June 1922

APPENDIX III

PRIMARY AND SECONDARY SOURCES

A summary of the primary and some of the secondary sources for the study of the Birmingham Triennial Musical Festivals available in Birmingham Central Library

LSH	Local Studies and History Department
ML	Music Library
ARCH	Birmingham City Archives

LSH	Complete run of Festival Programme books - some later ones autographed (some duplicates in ML)
LSH & ML	Copies of nearly all the vocal scores of Festival choral commissions.
ML	Copies of some full scores and some performance materials
ARCH	MS 1292 Correspondence to Joseph Moore (director of the Festivals) relating to the administration of the Festivals during the first half of the nineteenth century
"	MS 1292/5 Series of 6 letters from Mendelssohn to Joseph Moore concerning commissioning, composition and performance of 'Elijah'. In English
"	MS 1470 Ephemera from the Festivals found at the Town Hall - mostly concerning administration and financial matters. With correspondence from the period 1860-80
"	MS 1472 Replies to requests for vice presidents 1887-8
"	MS 1552/1 Peyton's autograph book
"	MS 1596 Series of 4 letters from Bruch to Richard Peyton concerning 'The Lay of the Bell'. In German and French with English translations
"	MS 1774 Copy photograph of the people involved in the first performance of Sterndale Bennett's 'The Woman of Samaria' in 1867
"	LEE CROWDER 1171 Collection of letters to Robert Harding Milward from many Festival composers and artistes including a series from Gounod (in French), Stanford, Benedict, Cowen, Costa et al. Mostly dating from the first half of the 1880s
"	MS 1721 Manuscript of the original 1846 version of Mendelssohn's 'Elijah' as used at the first performance (ML)

" MS 2067 Documents stating the financial
arrangements for the first performance of
Gounod's 'Redemption' signed by Gounod,
Harding Milward, Henry and Alfred Littleton
and the assignment of copyright to Novello
(ML)

" MS 2067 Note in Gounod's hand
acknowledging the receipt of Fr 100,000 for
the assignment of rights for 'Mors et Vita' to
Novello (ML)

" MS 2067 Collection of approx. 200 letters,
notes and telegrams to Novello (Alfred
Littleton, August Jaeger, Henry Clayton) from
variously Elgar, G.H. Johnstone, William Dodd
and others regarding financial and other
practical matters relating to 'The Dream of
Gerontius', 'The Apostles' and 'The Kingdom'

This collection is in the process of being sorted
and catalogued and some items require
conservation so access may be restricted:
anyone proposing to consult these items
should contact the library in advance.